LET'S VISIT SPAIN

Let's visit
SPAIN

RONALD SETH

BURKE

ACKNOWLEDGEMENTS

The author and publishers are grateful to the following organisations and individuals for permission to reproduce copyright photographs in this book and to Garry Lyle for assistance in preparing this revised new edition:

J. Allan Cash; Colorific Photo Library Ltd; Douglas Dickins; Robert Estall; Hewett Street Studios; S. J. Orwell; The Spanish National Tourist Office; Travel Photo International and Alan W. Ward.

The cover photo of a Spaniard and his donkey against the background of the city of Toledo is reproduced by permission of Camera Press Ltd.

CIP data
Seth, Ronald
    Let's visit Spain – 2nd ed.
    1. Spain – Social life and customs – Juvenile literature
    I. Title
    946.083   DP48
ISBN 0 222 01025 8

Burke Publishing Company Limited
Pegasus House, 116–120 Golden Lane, London EC1Y 0TL, England.
Burke Publishing (Canada) Limited
Registered Office: 20 Queen Street West, Suite 3000, Box 30, Toronto, Canada M5H 1V5.
Burke Publishing Company Inc.
Registered Office: 333 State Street, PO Box 1740, Bridgeport, Connecticut 06601, U.S.A.
Typeset in "Monophoto" Baskerville by Green Gates Studios Ltd., Hull, England.
Printed in Singapore by Tien Wah Press (Pte.) Ltd.

Contents

SPAIN

ATLANTIC OCEAN

N

Corunna

ASTURIAS   CANTABRIA   BASQU
                                 COUN

GALICIA

LA
RIOJ

R.Douro

CASTILLA-LEON

PORTUGAL

□ Madrid

R.Tagus

EXTREMADURA   o Toledo CASTILLA
                                 CASTILLA

R. Gaudiana

o Jerez de los Caballeros

R. Guadalquivir

A N D A L U S I A

o Seville

o Granada

Jerez de la Frontera
            Malaga o
o Cadiz

Costa del So

o Gibraltar

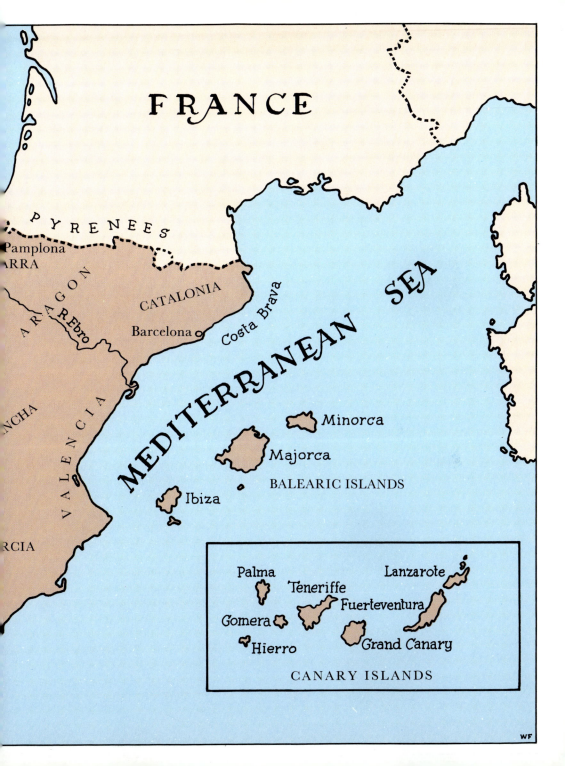

FRANCE

PYRENEES

Pamplona

ARRA

ARAGON

R. Ebro

CATALONIA

Barcelona

Costa Brava

MEDITERRANEAN SEA

NCHA

VALENCIA

Minorca

Majorca

BALEARIC ISLANDS

Ibiza

RCIA

Palma

Teneriffe

Lanzarote

Fuerteventura

Gomera

Hierro

Grand Canary

CANARY ISLANDS

WF

The Square Country

Like Italy, which looks like a leg about to kick a football (Sicily), Spain has its own special shape. If you allow for a bulge here and a dent there, and for a large chunk taken out of one side to make Portugal, it is almost square.

Spain and Portugal together are often called the Iberian Peninsula—from Iberia, the name which the Ancient Greeks gave it. Its coasts are washed by the Atlantic Ocean in the north and west, and by the Mediterranean Sea in the south and east. And though it is joined to the rest of Europe along the French frontier in the north-east, it is almost cut off from France by the Pyrenees mountains. Only at either end of the Pyrenees are there narrow gaps between the mountains and the sea through which roads and railways run into France.

Except for narrow stretches along the coasts, the whole of the country is one huge plateau, known as the *meseta*, which rises between about 370 metres (1,200 feet) and 920 metres (3,000 feet) above the sea, with an average height of 600 metres (2,000 feet). Rising out of the *meseta* are high mountain ranges which often reach a height of 2,400 metres (7,800 feet).

The plateau is cut by a number of large rivers, such as the Guadalquivir, the Gaudiana, the Douro, the Ebro and the Tagus. The longest river is the Tagus, which is 909 kilometres (565 miles) in length. After flowing for 600 kilometres (373 miles) through Spain, it enters Portugal, and flows into the Atlantic at Lisbon, the Portuguese capital.

Besides these main rivers, there is a vast number of smaller

A hillside village in the Pyrenees

ones. Despite this, however, large parts of Spain still have to be irrigated. This is because neither the winter rains nor the melting snow from the mountains provide sufficient water in summer.

Spain has a curious variety of climates. The *meseta*, especially around Madrid, the capital (which is in the centre of the country), is the sunniest area in Europe. It is also the driest part of Europe west of Russia, and it suffers badly from summer droughts. In Madrid, the summer temperature is around 38 degrees Centigrade (100 degrees Fahrenheit) in the shade, though the nights are cold; though the city is much further south than Rome, it is often possible to skate there in January.

In the south of Spain there are no such great contrasts of heat and cold. The climate all along the south and east coasts is what we call "Mediterranean"; the summers are not so hot as in Madrid, and the winters are pleasantly mild.

Parts of the *meseta* are so dry that they are semi-desert heathlands where no trees will grow. But there are also plains which are quite like the steppes of Russia, where wheat, esparto grass and olives are grown. Vines grow in the valleys of the great rivers, while oranges, lemons, figs, pomegranates and rice are cultivated in the irrigated areas.

Because of the many mountains and valleys, there are not very many roads and railways in Spain. Though more than twice the size of Great Britain, it has only 13,533 kilometres (8,410 miles) of railway to Great Britain's 17,427 kilometres (10,831 miles), and 147,963 kilometres (91,960 miles) of

The fruit and vegetables on sale in this street market are typical of the variety and quality of the produce of fertile areas of the country

roads to Great Britain's 212,501 kilometres (132,070 miles).

Almost 40,000,000 people live in Spain, which allows 75 people for each square kilometre (less than half a square mile).

Spain's Past

Spain has been inhabited from the earliest times. A skull has been found not far from Gibraltar which belonged to a man who lived probably 45,000 years ago. In some caves in northern Spain, there are several hundred wall-paintings and engravings drawn by men who lived at the same time.

The recorded history of Spain, however, begins round about 1100 B.C. The Phoenicians, who lived where the country of Lebanon is today, were great traders. They sailed the Mediterranean, setting up trading-posts along the coast of North Africa, in Sicily, Italy and Spain.

Not long after the Phoenicians, the Greeks arrived in Spain. Both set up colonies along the southern coast, but did not go far inland. Later, however, people from Carthage, in North Africa (another great Phoenician trading colony) came to Spain. Originally, they came to help their fellow-countrymen there. But they stayed, travelled inland, and made large parts of southern Spain rich and prosperous.

Little by little, the Greeks lost their great empire and, at the same time, the Romans began to grow more and more powerful. They were determined to control all the Mediterranean. As the Carthaginians both in Carthage and Spain were their only rivals, they decided to destroy them. There was one great war, which began in 264 B.C. and lasted for twenty-three years.

Though the Carthaginians were driven out of Sicily at the end of this war, they were by no means defeated. For the next thirty years they made an even greater effort to increase their colonies in Spain, to compensate for the loss of Sicily.

The Romans could not allow this, so they declared war on the Carthaginians again, in 218 B.C. By 200 B.C. they had driven the Carthaginians out of Spain, and had taken over the country themselves.

The Romans governed Spain for 650 years. By the end of this time, they were beginning to lose their power and, with it, their great empire. They were attacked in Spain by the German warrior tribes, the most powerful of whom were the Vandals. Since they could not defend themselves against the Vandals, the Romans asked another German warrior tribe, the Visigoths, to help them. But the Romans might as well have given in to the Vandals, for the Visigoths decided to stay and they eventually took Spain for themselves.

The Visigoths ruled Spain for about two hundred years. Then they began to quarrel among themselves about which religion should be the religion of Spain. A war broke out, and one side asked Muslims from North Africa and Palestine to come and help them. The first Muslims were followed by others. Soon the Muslims took over Spain for themselves.

These Muslims, known as the Moors, ruled the country. From time to time, the Spanish Christians went to war against the Moors, but it was not until the thirteenth century that the Christians began to get the upper hand.

One of the great champions in the struggle against the Moors was El Cid, whose great personal courage, skill as a leader of troops and military successes won him a fabulous reputation among Moors and Christians alike. Unfortunately, when he died in 1099, most of the country he had gained from the Moors was won back by them.

Just over a century later, however, the only territory still under the Moors was the province of Granada. By this time, Spain was divided into two Christian kingdoms—Aragon and Castile. The rulers of these two kingdoms were often at war with one another but, in 1474, the Queen of Castile, Isabella, married King Ferdinand of Aragon. When Isabella died, five years later, Ferdinand became king of united Spain.

In 1492, the year that Columbus discovered America, Ferdinand drove the last Moors out of Spain. Already, under

Some of the 850 columns of the Cordoba mosque. This relic of the Muslim occupation of Spain dates back to the eighth century

the joint rule of Isabella and Ferdinand, Spain had begun to be a great nation. With the discovery of the New World, she was to become one of the most wealthy and powerful countries of Europe, for Spanish ships sailed to North and South America and came back groaning under the weight of gold, silver and precious jewels, which Spanish soldiers took from the native inhabitants of the newly found territories.

Early in the next century—in 1516—King Charles I of Spain became the ruler of a huge empire, which included Holland and Belgium, Sicily, much of Italy and the southern part of North America—not only Mexico, but also a considerable part

15

A remarkable fourteenth-century castle in Castile

of what is now the United States. In addition, there were large possessions in South America, which had been divided between Spain and Portugal by the Pope, as well as colonies in India, the Far East and Africa. Spain was, therefore, one of the richest countries in the world.

Philip II of Spain married the English Queen Mary Tudor. When she died, he proposed marriage to Queen Elizabeth I, but she refused to have him for her husband. Philip was determined to make Britain part of his empire and, in 1588, he sent a large fleet, the Great Armada, to invade England. Sir Francis Drake and his sailors prevented the ships from landing the Spanish soldiers, and those ships which the English did not sink were destroyed by a great storm.

During Philip's reign, Spain's power and wealth began to decline, partly because of war, and partly because the riches brought from the New World made the Spaniards uninterested in work. When King Charles II died, in 1700, a French prince

16

of the Bourbon family became King of Spain. In trying to bring back Spain's former glory, his successors became the partners of the French in several wars.

Napoleon, however, quarrelled with Spain, turned out the Spanish Bourbon king, and made his own brother king instead. The Spaniards then became allies of Britain. The great British general, the Duke of Wellington, fought the French in Spain and defeated them a year before the Battle of Waterloo (1815).

The House of Bourbon was then restored to the Spanish throne and Ferdinand VII became king. During Ferdinand's reign, Spain's American colonies, which had broken away from Spain some years earlier, formed themselves into independent republics. When Ferdinand died, in 1838, a civil war broke out between the supporters of his daughter Isabella and those of her uncle, Don Carlos. It ended with a victory for Isabella. For almost a century, though there were periods of peace, Spain was in a state of great unrest.

Spain did not take part in the First World War but, in 1921, the Spanish army was badly defeated while trying to stop a rebellion in Spanish Morocco, in North Africa. The result was a struggle between the politicians and the army which ended in a military revolt led by General Primo de Rivera. Rivera became prime minister and ruled the country as a dictator, though the king, Alfonso XIII, remained as a figure-head. However, elections in 1931 were won by parties opposed to the king. He abdicated and the country became a republic.

Still unrest continued. The opposing political parties, the Communists and the extreme right-wing Fascists, were constantly organising revolts and strikes. This unhappy situation came to a head in 1936 when the part of the army which was in Morocco, led by General Franco, rose in revolt. When Franco had taken over Morocco, he moved with his forces to Spain. Soon a terrible civil war was raging, in which both democratic and communist forces opposed Franco.

The civil war continued until the end of March 1939. It resulted in a victory for Franco who set up another dictatorship with himself as *El Caudillo*—the Leader.

Spain did not take part in the Second World War, though Franco favoured the Germans and Italians.

Franco ruled Spain for nearly forty years. During that time, he promised that the monarchy would be restored when his rule ended, and he chose Prince Juan Carlos to be the first of the new kings.

Prince Juan Carlos, a grandson of the king who abdicated in 1931, became King Juan Carlos I when Franco died in 1975. Many people thought that he would be only a figurehead for another Fascist government, but they were mistaken. Early in his reign, free parliamentary elections were held, and an attempted return to Fascism by force in 1981 was a failure. Largely because the king himself took a firm stand against the rebels, they surrendered after less than one day.

In the 505,000 square kilometres (195,000 square miles) that make up Spain there are several different kinds of Spaniards. Those who live in Castile, in the centre of the country, are looked upon as typical Spaniards. They inhabit a dry part of the country which does not produce much, and it was they who were most involved in the struggle against the Moors. These two facts seem to have made them less open in manner and more simple in their desires than, for example, the people of the south. They are also very sensitive and proud.

Those who live in Galicia, in the north-west corner, are hard-working mountain people, quite different from those who live in Catalonia, on the other side of the country, and who are active, seafaring businessmen. The Andalusians, in the south, are different from any of these. It was their part of the country which was most influenced by the Romans and the Moors and, compared with the others, they are soft and pleasure-loving.

But, wherever you go in Spain, the thing that probably strikes you most is the music. Everywhere, and seemingly at all times, guitars are being strummed and people are singing. From this, you would say that the Spaniards are a happy people, and it makes you wonder why they have had such a long history of fighting one another.

How the Spaniards Make their Living

More than one-quarter of all Spaniards depend on the land for their living, despite the fact that most of it is parched and poor. In fact, really good soil is to be found only in certain small irrigated areas around the edges of the peninsula.

Changes in agricultural methods might have improved some of the land, but unfortunately many of the great landowners in the past refused to do anything to develop it. Much of the best land was owned by the Church and the nobles, who preferred sheep-farming to agriculture because it was cheaper and provided better profits. Though he realised that this was a great drawback to developing Spain as a whole, General Franco met so much resistance to his plans to improve the situation that he was not very successful.

As much to blame as the climate, which makes at least two-thirds of all Spain so poor and dry, and as the refusal of the landowners to make improvements, were the long conflicts that the Spaniards were constantly waging among themselves. A man who is always fighting has little time to work on the land; and wars, even civil wars, are so expensive that there was no money to carry out improvements. For example, plans for large schemes of irrigation had long been in existence before Spain became a republic in 1931, but there was never any money to start on them; and the great Civil War (1936–1939) put back the clock even further. Agriculturally, Spain is still one of the least productive countries of Europe, because of the lack of fertilisers, and much of the work is done by hand because many farmers cannot afford to buy machines.

However, up to the time of the Civil War, Spain did manage to produce all the cereals she needed for her own use.

20

But, after the war, many farmers stopped growing cereals because Franco's government fixed prices in order to keep down the cost of food. They switched to crops like cotton, tobacco, vegetables and fruit, whose prices were not controlled and which, therefore, gave them a better profit. Spain now has to import considerable quantities of cereals, particularly of maize. But in recent years cereal production has begun to increase again.

Among the most profitable of the agricultural crops is olives. Most of them are grown in Andalusia, though there are other important olive-growing areas in Catalonia, Castile and Estremadura. Nearly all the olive crop is turned into olive oil, much of which is exported.

Wine is another important source of agricultural income. There are large vineyards in many parts of Spain, especially in Catalonia, Valencia and Malaga. These produce table wines, while sherry and brandy are produced in the south-west.

The olive harvest. When the olives are ripe, they are knocked from the trees by men and women using long poles. The olives are then used to make olive oil

In many parts of Spain farmers are still working poor soil with outdated methods. This kind of wooden plough is a common sight in country districts

Fruit-growing is second only to cereal-raising. Oranges and lemons are the most important crops. A specially bitter orange is grown round Seville. It ripens in January and February and large quantities are exported to Britain, where they are used in making the orange jam known as marmalade. Nearly all British marmalade is made from Seville oranges. Stoned fruits, soft fruits and vegetables are dried or tinned and also exported.

The Spaniards eat a good deal of rice, and Spain produces more of it than any other country in Europe except Italy. One of the best kinds of onions—the well-known Spanish onion—is also grown in large quantities; and some are exported.

Certain crops, like esparto—a grass used in paper-making—hemp, flax and cotton are known as "industrial crops".

22

These, including tobacco, which is grown chiefly in Granada, increased greatly while the production of cereals was decreasing. The most important industrial food crops are sugar cane and sugar beet. Large quantities of all these are exported. They bring to Spain the much-needed foreign income with which she can buy those things which she cannot produce herself.

Animals still play a large part in Spanish agricultural life, because methods of tilling are primitive, roads are bad and tractors are too expensive for farmers. Ploughing is often done by cows or oxen, while mules and asses are used to draw carts.

Sheep are bred in all parts of the country. The two chief breeds are the churro and the merino. The wool of the churro is long and coarse, but the fleece of the merino is curly and

Sheep grazing in an olive grove

Cutting sugar cane

silky and produces a very fine white wool. For many years merino sheep were bred only in Spain.

There is hardly any dairy-farming in Spain. What there is, is in the north and the north-west.

*   *   *

Spain has a coastline of nearly 3,200 kilometres (1,965 miles) but unfortunately, there are very few good natural harbours, except in Galicia, in the north-west corner. Most of the fishing is done here. The catches include sardines—which are

24

tinned and exported in large quantities—anchovies, hake, tunny and shellfish.

Quite a large area of Spain is covered by pine, oak, beech and poplar forests and woodlands. Nearly all the cork in the world is produced by Spain, from the cork oak which is grown in Andalusia and Catalonia.

Spain is also very rich in minerals, including oil. At one time, before copper, lead, mercury and iron ore were discovered outside Europe, Spain was one of the world's leading producers of these minerals. But it is the same story here as with agriculture. The constant civil wars and the lack of money to develop the mining of these minerals brought about a serious decline in their production. However, the output is now increasing.

A typical Spanish trawler

Spain's other industries are to be found in a number of small areas which are islands in a sea of agriculture. By far the most important of these areas is Catalonia, where the chief product is textiles. Ninety per cent of the cotton, seventy-five per cent of the wool and most of the rayon are spun there.

Since the Second World War, tourism has become an extremely important source of income for the Spaniards.

Before the Second World War it was the well-off or more adventurous who went abroad for their holidays. Nowadays, with package holidays and cheap flights, hundreds of thousands of tourists visit the countries of Europe every summer in search of the sun, and large numbers of them go to Spain.

Foreigners go to Spain for their holidays chiefly because the cost of living there is much lower than in any other country in western Europe except, perhaps, Portugal and Greece. This means that hotels and other holiday attractions are also cheap. People from Britain and other northern countries are also attracted, of course, by the glorious sunny summers, especially on the Mediterranean coast. For those who are interested in historical buildings and in old paintings there is also much to see.

The most popular part of Spain is the Mediterranean coast, particularly those stretches to the north and south of Barcelona. From Barcelona to the French frontier is the Costa Brava— the rugged coast. To the south, as far as Cadiz, is the Costa del Sol—the coast of the sun.

The Costa del Sol previously had a number of resorts to

which the Spaniards used to go for their holidays, such as Malaga, Alicante and Valencia. The Costa Brava, however, consisted mostly of little fishing villages.

But mainly because it was much closer to the countries of northern Europe, the Costa Brava attracted most foreign holidaymakers; and the Spaniards, who realised what the tourist trade could mean to them, quickly went into action. Take, for instance, Tossa del Mar. Thirty years ago, Tossa was a little fishing village. Now there are numerous sky-scraper hotels, fishing is scarcely noticed, and the little

Tourists in the sun near Malaga. This modern hotel was built by the Spanish government

village has become a booming seaside resort for foreigners.

What has happened to Tossa has happened to many other villages as well.

The Spaniards and How They Live

In all large countries, the people of one region differ in character from those in others, but this is particularly true in Spain.

The Castilians who live in Castile, the province in the centre of the country in which most of the high plateau of the *meseta* is situated, look upon themselves as the true Spaniards. They are lean and dark, and have sombre faces which make them seem serious and reserved people. The language they speak is regarded as the purest form of Spanish.

Quite different are the Catalans who live in Catalonia, in the north-eastern corner, just below the Pyrenees. They are happier, jollier and much more lively than the Castilians. They also have a much more independent outlook and this makes them often impatient of what the central government in Madrid says must be done. They are more revolutionary than any other Spaniards.

The people of Andalusia, the province in the south, are quite different from either the Catalans or the Castilians.

28

They are easy-going and never over-anxious to get anything done. Their favourite word is *mañana*—tomorrow, we'll do it tomorrow; and, of course, tomorrow never comes.

Andalusia is really typical of what we imagine all Spain to be like. It is the country of castanets and guitar music, of singing barbers and of wild *flamenco* songs and dances. Of course, for many years all these things have been found in other parts of Spain, too. But they, and bullfighting, all began in Andalusia and were then taken up by people throughout the country.

The Galicians are quite different again. They live in the north-west corner of Spain and are a tough and hardy people. They are made so by the harsher climate which the winds of the Atlantic Ocean and the Bay of Biscay force on this part of the peninsula. General Franco, who led the Nationalists (Fascists) in the Civil War, and became Head of State when they won in 1939, was born and grew up in Galicia.

At the opposite end of the northern coast, just under the Pyrenees, live the Basques. Fiercely courageous and obstinate, they speak an ancient language of their own, which seems to be mostly spelled with the letters x and z by the sound of it.

Although Spain has so many different types of people, no matter where you find a Spaniard you can be sure that he will be polite, kind and hospitable. All Spaniards love and spoil their children, and are proud of their ancient tradition of good manners and courtesy.

Probably no other people in Europe take so much trouble

"Flamenco."
These songs
and dances
originated in
Andalusia but
have spread
throughout
Spain

over their appearance. Though they wear old clothes for work, the country people dress themselves in their best at all other times. They take the greatest care of their shoes, which have a very high shine. This, they say, is one of the signs of the *hidalgo*—the nobleman.

*   *   *

Whether they live in country villages or in the towns, except for breakfast, which they eat early so that they can do as much work as possible before the heat of the day, the Spaniards take their meals much later than the other peoples of western

30

Europe. The midday meal usually begins at about two o'clock and may go on till after four.

After lunch all Spain stops for the *siesta*—the afternoon rest. Everyone takes a siesta for two or three hours, in order to escape the hottest part of the day. Then, at around six o'clock, the country begins to come to life again. Shops, which have been closed, reopen and stay open until eight o'clock; and people who work in offices return and do another hour or two's work.

Between eight and ten o'clock is the time for the *paseo*, the evening promenade. Smartly-dressed groups of women and girls walk up and down the broad pavements or in the squares, passing and repassing groups of men and boys with whom they exchange glances and smiles. They are watched by men and women sitting in the pavement cafés, sipping sherry and nibbling snacks.

Except for the very rich, nearly all entertaining in Spain is done at the cafés. It is said that few foreigners have seen inside a Spanish home, no matter how close their friendship with a Spaniard may be. The evening meal rarely begins before ten o'clock, and it may last until midnight. Consequently cinemas and theatres and other places of entertainment seldom open before eleven o'clock.

Spain is a Roman Catholic country, and there are many religious holidays during the year. These holidays are great opportunities for putting on one's best clothes and promenading or going to the bull-fight, or taking part in special festivities.

All Spaniards are known by both their father's and their mother's surname. Thus, if your father's name was Robinson and your mother's Brown, and your first name was Alfred, you would be known as Señor Alfred Robinson y Brown; if you were a woman, you would take the names of your parents (if unmarried) or your husband (if married). (*Señor* = Mr; *Señora* = Mrs; *Señorina* = Miss; *y* = and). There is also a more formal way of addressing people. Instead of Señor and Señora, you say Don and Doña with the first name; e.g., Don Antonio and Doña Maria. These two titles were once only

32

given to the nobility, but nowadays they are widely used, especially when you want to show respect.

Until fairly recently the upbringing of young Spanish girls was very strict. No girl was allowed to be alone with a young man until they became engaged. An older woman, known as the *duenna* (chaperone), always sat in the same room with them. This custom has almost completely disappeared nowadays, especially in cities and towns visited by large numbers of foreign tourists. In some of the country places, however, it is still strictly observed.

The Spaniards love talking; in the villages as well as the towns, old friends will meet in a bar or café in the evenings

A typical village street

between six o'clock and dinner-time. Over a glass of sherry, they will discuss and argue about bull-fighting, football and politics, setting the whole world to rights.

Wherever you go in some countries the houses look pretty much the same. Not so in Spain. In the hot south, especially in Andalusia, the houses are almost African in style. Built of thick stone walls and with only a few windows, to keep out the intense heat of summer, they have tiled roofs and arched covered terraces. In fact, life in Andalusia is lived mostly out of doors. The houses are used only for sleeping and for shelter when the weather is bad. The houses of the rich are always built round a courtyard, and it is in the courtyard that meals are served, and the family sit and chat.

Houses in the hot south. They have thick walls and few windows, to keep out the heat of the sun

The courtyard of a more luxurious house

In Galicia, in the north, the houses are more lived in, because of the weather. However, nearly every house has a balcony, called a *mirador*, which has glass walls on three sides to protect the family from the Atlantic winds as they sit in the sun. Castilian houses are not quite so Moorish-looking as Andalusian houses, nor as solid as those of Galicia.

Practically every Spanish village has a square, which is the centre of village life. The church usually forms one side of it, and the bars and cafés will always be found there. The Spaniards are a sociable people, and they like nothing better than to be in a group.

35

This is also true of Spanish family life. Almost without exception, the grandparents live with one or other of their children, and two or three brothers, with their families, will often live together in the same house. As Spanish families have large numbers of children, the sharing of a house by several relatives means that life has very few dull moments.

There are still quite large areas of Spain which have no electricity but, even when it is available, many people still prefer to cook by the old-fashioned charcoal stove. As with the people themselves, their houses and the country they live in, Spanish food varies from region to region. In the north, they are very fond of stews; in the central regions the favourite is roasts; while in the south the preference is for dishes fried in olive-oil.

The best known of all Spanish dishes—especially now that you can buy it outside Spain in frozen-food stores—is *paella*. Actually *paella* means "a large iron frying-pan", and when you know what goes into it, you will realise why the pan has to be large.

Here is a very good *paella* recipe. Heat some olive-oil in the pan. Into it drop two sliced onions, which you fry until they are golden in colour. Add one chopped clove of garlic, two chopped red or green pimentoes (peppers), twelve stoned black olives and a few chicken livers. Mix them all up together, and see that there is still some oil in the pan. Now pour over this mixture twelve ounces (350 grammes) of rice, and fry it until it has soaked up all the oil. Add the flesh of one small

36

cooked lobster, half a litre (one pint) each of mussels and prawns, a few pieces of cooked white fish and four sliced tomatoes. Pour over this quarter of a litre (half a pint) of boiling water in which a little saffron has been dissolved. Simmer over a low heat until the rice is tender, which should be when all the water has evaporated. Serve it at once from the pan. With these quantities you should have enough for six people.

Another very popular dish all over Spain is a red peppery sausage called *chorizo*, and just as popular is a soup called *gazpacho*. *Gazpacho*, which was originally eaten only in Andalusia, is made from chopped tomatoes, cucumber, onions, green peppers and breadcrumbs, cooked in oil and vinegar flavoured with garlic. In hot weather it is served chilled, decorated with mayonnaise.

Spanish meat dishes are made from beef, veal and goat, but not much mutton is eaten. What the Spaniards really like is shellfish; fortunately they have quite a variety—shrimps, lobsters, crabs, crayfish, prawns and mussels. They eat them as snacks in between meals, washed down by sherry—the most famous of all Spanish wines.

Besides sherry, Spain produces many other wines, and a very good brandy. The wines, which have been given French names—e.g. Spanish *Graves*, Spanish *Chablis*, etc.—are sweeter than French wines.

Because of the many mountains in Spain, it is not always easy to get from one place to another. The trains, which run on a wide gauge railway, move slowly when compared with trains in the rest of Europe. There are only two or three real expresses which are drawn by up-to-date diesel locomotives; they run between Madrid and the other large cities.

In the country districts most of the transport is provided by mules, donkeys and oxen. Nowadays, buses are being used more widely for carrying people from the villages into the towns. If you ever want to have a hair-raising experience, go for a ride in a Spanish country bus.

With their complete disregard for time, their long *siestas* and their many holidays and *fiestas*, the Spaniards may give the impression that they are lazy people, but they are, in fact, very hard-working. There are some very rich families in

Paella, the best known of all Spanish dishes

Spain, but most Spaniards are not well off compared with the
people of other countries in Western Europe, and those who
work on the land are often very poor. They have to work hard
in order to live.

In the cities, much of the business is done in the cafés over a
glass of sherry or light beer, or a cup of coffee. If you go to
Spain and see the cafés crowded with men in the mornings and
early evenings, they are more likely to be making important
deals than discussing the chances of the Real Madrid football
team in the European Cup.

Schools and Universities

Although primary education is compulsory in Spain, quite a number of Spanish children never go to school. Despite the many schools which have been built since the end of the Civil War, there are still not enough to go round. This is especially true of the remote villages.

The Moors, who ruled the country from 715 to 1492, were very keen on education and built many schools. When they were at last driven out by King Ferdinand and Queen Isabella, the Roman Catholic Church, which has always been powerful in Spain, took over in the field of education. Until the Civil War, nearly every school in Spain belonged to the Church. Now the government is responsible for most of the primary schools, though there are a number run by private concerns.

By law, Spanish children must attend school from the age of six until they are fourteen—if there is a school for them to go to. Boys and girls must be taught in separate schools, except in places with a very small population.

All primary education is free, though there are a number of fee-paying private schools to which parents may send their children, if they wish. The State has considerable control over what is taught and how it is taught. Instruction must be given in Castilian Spanish which is regarded as the "true" Spanish. All schools use the same textbooks, which have been approved by the Ministry of Education.

40

In the villages and smaller towns, there is a great temptation for the poorer families not to send their children to school, because every pair of hands which can be put to work in the fields or in other jobs, means more money for the family. However, if any parent deliberately makes a child take a job instead of sending him to school, or if anyone employs a child under the age of fourteen, both parent and employer may be severely punished.

When children are fourteen, they take an examination to find out whether they are suitable pupils for secondary education. If they pass successfully, and wish to continue at school until they are sixteen, they transfer immediately to their secondary school.

At sixteen, they take another examination to see if they should go to university. If they pass, they stay on at school for another year and take a special course, with a university entrance examination at the end of it. If they fail this examination, they are allowed to take it again, two or three times. The books used in this university entrance course can be chosen by the pupils and teachers, but they have to have the approval of the Ministry of Education.

More than half the secondary schools are run by the Church, and one-quarter are private schools. Pupils attending these schools have to pay fees, but the remaining quarter, which are State schools, are free.

Spain has thirty-three universities, some of which are very old. The oldest is at Salamanca, in the region of Leon; it was

founded nearly seven hundred and fifty years ago, in A.D. 1230, and so is nineteen years older than Oxford, the oldest British university.

Twenty-five of the universities are run by the State, which chooses the rectors (the heads) and the teachers. Students have to pay fees to attend a university, but the fees are quite low. For a population of less than 40,000,000, the figure of nearly 500,000 university students is high.

Madrid has the largest university, which is housed in a "city" of its own on the outskirts of the city. It has eighteen

42

thousand students. During the Civil War it was almost completely destroyed but it has since been rebuilt and enlarged. The students live in hostels in the University City which, besides lecture-halls and laboratories, also has swimming pools, theatres, cinemas and cafés.

Besides the University City, Madrid has another, smaller university which was founded in 1969, at the time when a second university was also founded in Barcelona. These two new universities are allowed to look after their own affairs, but they must get the approval of the State for any decision they may take. The only Spanish universities which are not controlled by the State in any way are four private universities, all controlled by the Roman Catholic Church.

Except among the poorer families, Spanish boys and girls take their education very seriously. They have to work very hard to obtain the certificates of education which all must have, with a few exceptions, before they can get a job.

In the summer, Spanish school and university holidays stretch from the middle of July to the middle of September, covering the hottest months of the year, when sweating over a desk would be very uncomfortable. Taken altogether, however, their holidays are several weeks shorter than those of some other European countries, including Britain.

The Spaniards at Play

Spain has twenty official public holidays. The Spaniards make good use of them, as they do of any leisure time that may come their way.

All over Spain, Sunday is always a real holiday. Nearly everyone goes to church early to hear Mass; once the Spaniards have done their religious duty, the rest of the day is fun. Cafés and restaurants are open; so are some of the shops in most of the cities. Mother and father and all the children, dressed in their best clothes, go together to walk in the park, have a drink in a café and, if they can afford it, lunch in a restaurant.

The Spanish people are mad about football, and there are always matches to be watched on a Sunday evening, after the heat of the day has passed. But the great, traditional pastime on a Sunday is the bullfight which, to most foreigners, seems an exceptionally cruel sport. But you have to remember that it is a man—compared with the bull, a tiny figure—who is pitting his skill against a ferocious animal, not with a gun but with a sword.

The most important *corridas de toros* (bullfights) take place in Madrid and Seville, where Spanish bullfighting originated; but every city and town of any importance now has its *plaza de toros* (bullring) in which there are bullfights on *fiesta* days, frequently on Sundays and on holidays during the summer. There are no bullfights in winter. The season opens with the Easter *corrida* at Seville, and goes on to the middle of October.

44

Bullfights always take place in the early evening. Even so, the early evening sun can be very hot. If you are wise, you will have paid a little extra and bought a ticket for a seat in the shade.

The *plaza de toros* is circular, hence its name bull*ring*. All round it are high banks of seats for the spectators. A wooden fence, standing a little way away from the first bank of seats, surrounds the ring. Behind it is a passage-way. In this *callejon*, as it is called, you will see various people making their preparations.

In the fence are four narrow openings, each protected by a wooden shield. The shield is built just far enough away from the opening to allow a man to squeeze through, but not a bull. These openings, each of which is in a different section of the fence, provide a refuge for the *toreros* (bullfighters) if a charging angry bull gets too near them.

The most important man at the bullfight is, of course, the *matador de toros* (which means "killer of bulls".) He is assisted by a number of other men in the early stages of the fight. They play the bull with their cloaks in order to tire him. If the bull comes too close, they leap behind the fence. For a *matador* to do so would be a disgrace which he would probably never be able to live down.

Most bullfights involve six bulls. Usually there will be three *matadors*, each of whom takes on two bulls—separately, of course—thus making six separate fights.

Much ancient traditional ceremony is connected with the

The ceremonial procession which begins the bullfight

corrida de toros. Under the spectators' seats are a number of rooms—dressing-rooms, hospital, and so on—one of which is a small chapel. Every *matador* goes to the chapel and prays that he will have a good fight and not be killed by the bull.

The entertainment begins with a ceremonial procession, led by two men on horseback, dressed in ancient historical costumes. Following them will come the three groups of *toreros*, first the *matador* and then the rest of his team. You can always tell the *matadores* by the splendid costumes they wear. They consist of a broad-shouldered short jacket made of brightly coloured silk or satin, beautifully decorated with spangles, gold thread and small jewels, and skin-tight, knee-length breeches of the same material also decorated along the

46

seams. Silk stockings, brilliantly shining shoes and a black three-cornered hat complete the costume, except for a wonderfully embroidered ceremonial cape—not used in fighting. *Matadores* wear their hair long, tied together in a short tail in the nape of the neck, above which a half-circle of satin-covered cork is fixed into the hair. The costumes of some of the famous *matadores* are very costly.

At the rear of the procession come gaily decorated teams of mules. They will drag the dead bull out of the ring at the end of each fight.

The mayor of the city or town is the president of the *corrida*. He sits with his friends in a box facing the bull-pen. The procession makes its way round the ring and stops in front of

"Matadores" in their brilliant costumes

the president's box. They all bow to him with a gallant sweep of their hats, and he throws down the key of the bull-pen. All those not taking part in the first fight leave the ring, the bull-pen is unlocked and the first bull rushes out. As he passes through the gate, an attendant sitting above it thrusts a small dagger into its shoulder muscles. Attached to the dagger is a rosette in the colours of the ranch where the bull was reared.

These bulls are not just ordinary bulls. They are specially bred for fighting from pedigree stock. At various stages of their young life they are tested for courage. If they do not prove to be really fierce they are killed for meat.

The fight itself is divided into three parts. However, before the first part begins, the *banderilleros*, one at a time, attract the bull with their capes so that the matador may judge whether the bull likes to attack with both horns, or with only one. After ten seconds of this, a bugle is blown to warn the *matador* that he must begin using the silken work cape and so lead the bull into the first act, so to speak.

When the matador has been working the bull with the cape for a while, the bugle is blown again, and the *picadores* come into the ring. The *picadores* are on horseback; on seeing the horse, the bull charges. The picador has to fend the bull off with sharp pointed lances, with the object of making him more and more angry. As the horses were very often horribly injured by the bull, since 1930 they have been protected by armour made of pressed cotton, leather and canvas.

48

After a time, the bugle announces the act of the *banderilleros*. The *picadores* leave the ring, and the *banderilleros* enter, armed with pairs of staves about 70 centimetres (27 inches) long, each with a metal dart at one end and coloured paper streamers flying from the other. These they plunge into the bull's shoulder where it joins the neck, in the exact position which the *matador* has pointed out.

Many people believe that these darts are thrust into the bull to make him angry. This is not the reason. Most bulls prefer to attack always with one horn, that is to say, always from the same side. The darts, which are quite heavy, are plunged into the side with which he does *not* attack, and this makes him attack equally from both sides.

When the darts have been planted, the bugle sounds again, this time to announce Act Three—the killing—which is known as the Hour of Truth. The *matador* alone makes the kill. The *banderilleros* stay in the ring, but only go to the assistance of the *matador* should he have an accident.

Before beginning the last act, the *matador* goes to the president's box. Holding his hat aloft in one hand and his *muleta* (cape) and *estoque* (sword) in the other, he asks the president's permission to dedicate the bull to a famous person present, or to a beautiful lady or a friend. When the president has given his permission, the *matador* tosses his hat to the person he has chosen. It is a great honour to have a bull dedicated to you and to receive the *matador*'s hat.

It is now that the *matador* shows his skill and courage as

a bullfighter. He has the skill to kill the bull quickly, but if he did so he would be greeted by howls of anger and jeers from the crowd. His real skill is to make the bull charge him and, by swerving to one side, to escape at the very last moment. Quite often the bull is so close to the *matador* as he rushes by that some of his hairs are found afterwards on the *matador*'s suit.

The moves the *matador* makes during the preparation for the kill are as carefully worked out as ballet steps are. Though most of them are traditional "passes"—as they are called— quite a number have been invented by famous *matadores*.

In order to satisfy the crowd's demand for a thrill, the *matador* deliberately faces great risks, of being either badly injured or killed, every time he faces a bull. The *matador*'s own life depends on his being able to persuade the bull to charge straight at his cape. In order to do this, the bull must have good eyesight; when accidents to the *matador* do happen, it is the bull's bad eyesight that is to blame. If the bull cannot see properly, at the very last moment he makes a move which the *matador* is not expecting. *Matadores* are not often killed or injured by bulls which charge straight. Those who are, are generally young *matadores*, without much experience, who lose their heads at the demands of the crowd, and try to be too clever.

To kill a bull certainly and cleanly, the *matador* has to thrust his sword into the great artery between the bull's shoulder blades which causes instant death without any bleeding. This is quite a small spot to hit; if the sword is not

50

thrust in correctly, it will bounce off. The crowd will greet this with shouts of disgust. The *matador* is allowed to try again, provided he follows the very strict rules laid down, but if he misses he will not be a favourite with the crowd.

Spaniards who go to the bullfights are mostly *afficionados*— experts. They know every move that should be made, and they are expert judges of the *matadores'* skills.

If a *matador* has put on a good performance, after circling the ring with his *banderilleros*, he will receive back his hat, in which will be a present of money. If his performance has been very good, he will also be given one of the bull's ears; if excellent, both ears. But if he has given an outstanding performance, he will receive both ears and the tail.

The great *matadores* are the idols of all Spaniards, and they can make large fortunes. They are the Spanish equivalent of film-stars.

Bullfights are held not only on Sundays and holidays, but on *fiesta* days as well, if there is a *plaza de toros* in the town or city where the *fiesta* is being held.

Fiesta means a *feast* or *festival*. As we know, Spain is a Roman Catholic country, and the Church sets aside certain days for celebrating one or other of the saints. Each church has its own patron saint, that is, the saint to whom the church has been dedicated and who, in return, will protect the church and the people who worship there.

Each patron saint has a special day in the year, when the people give thanks for the protection given to them in the past

51

Gypsy dancers in
Granada. The girl
in the centre is
only nine years
old

year, and ask for it to be continued in the coming year. On
these special days, a *fiesta* is arranged.

First, the people go to church and say their prayers of
thanks. At the end of the service, the figure of the saint—
every church has one—is carried in procession through the
streets with bands playing and the people following in
procession.

When the figure of the saint has been returned to the

52

church, the solemn part of the *fiesta* is over. The remainder of the day is spent in feasting, singing and dancing.

The best known Spanish dances are the *flamenco*. There are many different *flamenco* dances. Some are danced by men alone, some by women alone, and some by men and women together, though they never touch one another. The men wear a black round hat, a short jacket, tight-fitting trousers, and boots with high, blocked heels. The women wear silk dresses, with many rows of frills on the skirt, which swirls about as they dance. On their heads they wear a kind of lace shawl, known as the *mantilla*, fixed to the hair with high, beautiful combs.

The music is provided by guitars and singing. In fact, originally the *flamenco* were songs, and only later did people dance to them. There is much stamping of feet, especially in the men's dances called *zapateados*, a kind of tap dance, clicking of *castanets*—small pieces of wood hollowed out like shells, held in a special way by the dancers—clapping by the spectators and many shouts of *olé*.

Flamenco dancers have used the same steps for many hundreds of years. Like the bullfight *aficionados*, there are *flamenco aficionados*, too, who watch the dancers carefully. They know when the slightest mistake has been made, and they let the dancers know they know.

The best *flamenco* dancers nowadays are gypsies; it is probably for this reason that many people have the idea that it is a gypsy dance. It is, however, a true Spanish dance. Many people also think that the *flamenco* is the only Spanish dance.

In fact, all the regions have their own dances, though several have been "borrowed" by other regions.

There is, for example, the *sardana*, which is danced in all the towns and villages of Catalonia. It is a round dance, that is, danced in a circle. Though originally Catalan, the *sardana* is now a national dance. Then there is the *jota* which is danced in Aragon and Navarre, and the *sevillanos*, danced in Seville. These are quite different from the *flamenco*, as are the *bolero* and the *fandango*.

Guitars are as much part of everyday Spanish life as they are of the jollifications of the *fiesta*. Not all *fiestas* have religious beginnings. One of the best known non-religious is the *fallas*, which takes place in Valencia. Huge *papier mâché* figures are set up in the streets, and others are carried in processions. Some of them have heads which are the likenesses of prominent

Dancing the "Sardana" in Catalonia

local people. The processions at nearly all *fiestas* include decorated floats pulled by oxen. The people who take part in the processions wear the national costumes of the region.

One of the most famous of all Spanish *fiestas*, is the *fiesta* held in Seville on the day before Easter Sunday. A huge jewelled image of the Virgin Mary and groups showing the last days of Christ on earth, are carried through the streets on the shoulders of barefoot penitents carrying lighted candles. They wear long pointed black or white hoods over their heads and faces, with slits for eyes, which make them look very mysterious.

In Andalusia they have a *fiesta* called the *Romeria*, partly a pilgrimage and partly a picnic, which may go on for some days. The best known of these *fiestas* is the *Romeria de Rocio*, which starts at San Lucar, near Cadiz, at Whitsuntide. It begins with a procession of beautifully decorated waggons drawn by oxen going to the famous chapel of the Virgin Mary. The first of these waggons has been made into a shrine, decorated with flowers and candles. The statue of the Virgin is taken out of the chapel and placed in it, and it takes its place at the head of the procession. Behind it come the waggons of the pilgrims which have been made to look like the waggons of the early American settlers.

Other waggons join the procession as it leaves the city and makes its way through the countryside. Men and women riding donkeys and mules go with it, and there are also pilgrims on foot, carrying banners. At nightfall, the procession

stops and an encampment is formed. After a meal, the guitars strike up, and there is singing and dancing far into the night.

Next morning, the procession sets off again. The pilgrims do not return to San Lucar until the evening of the third day.

Another famous *fiesta* is held at Pamplona, in Navarre, on the Feast of San Firman in July. Pamplona has a huge bullring, which seats thirteen thousand people.

On San Firman's Day, the bulls which have been chosen for the next *corrida de toros* are set free in the streets. All the young

56

men of Pamplona run ahead of them. The young ladies of the city watch safely from their balconies. The young men show off their courage, by letting the bulls get near to them and then dodging their horns. Sometimes some of them become too daring, and every year the festival ends with a number of young men in hospital.

Besides bullfighting and a passion for football, the Spaniards have another national sport: *pelota*. It originated in the Basque region, but is now played in other parts of Spain as well.

Most churches in Spain are built in the village square, and *pelota* began by the older boys and young men hitting a ball against the wall of the church that had no windows in it.

The crowned and bejewelled figure of the Virgin Mary being carried in Seville's Holy Week procession

Playing pelota in a village square. The houses in the background are typical of the Basque region.

Nowadays, it is played on a specially built court, which has high walls, rather like a large squash court.

The game is played by two or four people. Originally the players used their bare hands, and some do so even now, but more usually they strap a kind of scoop made of basket-work onto their right hand. With the *clota*, as it is called, they catch the ball and hurl it against the main wall as hard as

58

they can, so that it bounces back as far as possible. The players play the ball in turn.

Pelota is a very strenuous game. Even the experts rarely have the strength to play it after they have reached the age of thirty.

Certainly, the Spaniards know how to enjoy their leisure time. Spain is probably the most musical country in Europe, and the people enjoy themselves perhaps more than most when they are not working, although in other ways their life may be very hard.

Madrid—the Capital

The city of Madrid is practically in the centre of Spain, high up on the *meseta* of Castile, about 640 metres (2,100 feet) above sea-level.

It has been the capital of Spain since Philip II, the husband of Queen Mary Tudor and the king who sent the Armada against England, moved his court there in 1560. Before that, Toledo was the capital.

Though the chief city for more than four hundred years, it is only since General Franco became Head of State in 1939, that

Madrid has become the largest city in the country with a population of just over 2,250,000. To bring the population up to this number, many of the surrounding villages have had to be brought inside the city boundaries, and a very large building scheme has provided fine modern shops, offices and blocks of flats.

During the Civil War (1936–1939) Madrid was in the middle of the fighting for nearly two years. Large areas were completely flattened by air-attacks and bombardments during the struggle; the new buildings have been put up on the sites of the ruins.

Madrid is almost completely surrounded by beautiful parks and gardens. The centre of the city has many wide streets, large squares, avenues and promenades. But, as in other ancient capital cities, there are districts where the streets are narrow and badly paved, and the houses are dingy and closely clustered together.

Right in the middle of the city is the square of the Puerta del Sol, the Gate of the Sun, so-called after a gate which stood there until 1510, and had a large sun carved on it. The Puerta del Sol is like the hub of a wheel, whose spokes are formed by the streets. It was once the centre of Madrid and the city's busiest spot. Since the enlargement of the city by General Franco, several other squares in other parts of the town have taken away some of its importance as a city centre.

The finest of the ten streets which run from the Puerta del Sol is the Calle de Alcala, which meets the magnificent Paseo del Prado, the Prado Promenade. Here are some of Madrid's most handsome buildings—the Bank of Spain on one corner and the General Post Office on the opposite corner, as well as the Prado museum and the Academy of the Spanish Language.

If you go in the opposite direction to the Calle de Alcala from the Puerta del Sol, up the Calle del Arenal you reach Madrid's largest square: the Plaza de la Republica, in front of the royal palace. Many consider this palace to be one of Madrid's chief glories. Though the whole of the palace is beautiful, the Throne Room is the most beautifully decorated. On its walls hang eight hundred tapestries, most of them Flemish, showing well-known scenes from legend and history. Madrid has a second royal palace, the Royal Palace of El Pardo, which is just outside the city. In the park near the El Pardo there are still wild boar and deer, and thousands upon thousands of partridges, though it is so close to the city.

Madrid's loveliest park is the Retiro, which is also the largest park in Europe. The Spaniards love to walk in the coolness of its shady avenues and by the large artificial lake. Almost everywhere you turn you will see seventeenth-century statues. The whole park is beautifully kept, especially the small circular rose-garden which is a mass of colour from April till Christmas.

Everyone who visits Madrid makes a point of visiting the Prado Museum. Spain has produced a number of great painters; El Greco (1541–1614), Velasquez (1599–1660) and Francisco de Goya (1746–1828) are the most famous and rank as Great Masters. In the Prado there are the finest collections of

61

The Royal Palace in Madrid

the paintings of these artists to be found anywhere in the world.

El Greco was a Greek (*El Greco* means "the Greek") who had been born in Crete, went to Italy and studied under Titian, the great Italian master, in Venice. In 1575 he went to Spain and settled in Toledo, then the capital. In 1580, or thereabouts, Philip II engaged him to paint a picture on the subject of St. Maurice and the Theban Legion. When the picture was finished it was quite different from any other picture painted in Spain up to that time. Its vivid colours and the tremendous feeling of life which El Greco was able to put into it so startled the king that he could not bear to look at it.

El Greco completely changed his style of painting when he had lived in Spain for a year or two. Though a foreigner, he is looked upon as a Spanish painter.

Diego Velasquez was a Spaniard. He was already a master by the time he was twenty when he painted the Adoration of the Magi which hangs in the Prado. He painted a number of Bible scenes, but he was also a great portrait painter. Indeed, there are few, if any, artists who can surpass him in this form of art.

Francisco de Goya was quite different from both El Greco and Velasquez. A strongly built man who loved living, he had for his friends both the beggars on the church steps and the noble ladies in their palaces. He painted three or four hundred portraits and a vast number of other pictures about every subject under the sun.

A view of the Prado Museum. The statue in front of it shows the painter Velasquez

He is best known, however, for his etchings (The Disasters of War) and for four drawings of the Bulls of Bordeaux. These are considered by experts to be unequalled by the work of any other artist.

Quite different from the Prado Museum is the Rastro, popularly known as the flea-market. Stalls line both sides of the street, and you can find really good bargains here if you know what you are looking for. But, take care, smooth-talking young men will offer you "gold" watches, famous makes of fountain pens, "diamond" rings and other valuable items, all for a song. Though they may look like the real thing, they are all fakes and practically valueless.

Madrid has many churches. Some are old and contain beautiful pictures and treasures. The chief church of Madrid, the Almudena cathedral, is fairly new, however. Standing between the Royal Palace and the smaller palace of the Infanta Maria Teresa, it was begun in 1880, and is not yet finished, though parts of it are in use.

The broad avenues and promenades of Madrid are lined with pavement cafés, where it is pleasant to sit and sip a glass of sherry or a long cooling drink, and watch the world go by. Or you can enjoy the evening *paseo*, strolling along one of the wide streets or in one of the many fine squares and parks.

When you have been to Madrid, you may agree that the most interesting sight of all is the Madrileños themselves, as the people who live there are called. They chatter without stopping and they laugh ceaselessly, always to an accompaniment of

64

guitar music and singing, though you may never see the musicians.

A mixture of very old and very new, Madrid still has a flavour all its own. There is no other city in Europe like it; the Madrileños know this, and are proud of it.

Other Cities

Barcelona

Spain has many other beautiful cities besides Madrid. They are all quite different from one another; each has a character all its own.

The most important city after the capital is Barcelona. It is the second largest city in Spain, with a population of 1,800,000. It is situated on the Mediterranean coast 160 kilometres (about one hundred miles) from the frontier with France.

Besides being a seaside resort, Barcelona is also a very important port, quite as important as the French port of Marseilles, and the Italian port of Genoa. It is an industrial centre, too, its chief products being textiles. Foreigners, and, in fact, other Spaniards tend to overlook the fact that its university, the Universidad Literaria, founded in 1430, is a great centre of learning. Its medical schools claim to produce the best doctors in Spain; this is certainly true of its eye-surgeons who are among the most skilful in the world.

The oldest part of the city is built on a small hill which the Romans called Monte Taber. The Roman walls can still be seen in the Via Layetana, which runs north from the Plaza Antonio Lopez, near the harbour. They can also be seen in other streets including the Avenida de la Catedral. A few years ago, when a new road had to be cut through a slum area, a really beautiful old house stood in the way. Instead of knocking it down, the council took it down stone by stone and rebuilt it in another place. As the new foundations for it were being dug, the workmen came upon remains of the Roman town, which they excavated and then protected by a cellar, over which they rebuilt the old house. You can now go down into this cellar and walk along part of a street along which Roman soldiers walked two thousand years ago.

The modern part of the city is noisy and thriving. At its centre is the Plaza Cataluna, with its great flocks of pigeons, like Trafalgar Square in London or St. Mark's Square in Venice. It is as busy as Piccadilly Circus.

On the sides of the hill which slopes up from the sea are the modern villas and apartment houses. At the bottom of the hill is the old town and the port.

The hill on which modern Barcelona is built is called

Rambla de las Flores, Barcelona

The Plaza Cataluna in the centre of modern Barcelona

Tibidabo, two Latin words meaning *Tibi*—"to you", *dabo*—"I will give". In the old days, the simple people in many countries believed that the events in the Gospels took place, not in Palestine, but in their own country. The people of Barcelona believed that this hill was the one to which the Devil took Jesus Christ and said to him, "If you will worship me *I will give to you* all that you can see from this spot."

To get from the modern city to the port you go down a long series of streets called the Ramblas. On both sides of these streets are open-air stalls, shaded by plane trees and huge umbrellas, stacked with flowers, fruit, vegetables and caged birds. Near the Ramblas is the covered market in which many of the stalls sell fish. Here you can buy tunny, live eels, turbot, haddock, soles, cod, salmon, lobsters, crabs, cockles, mussels

68

and oysters, all of which have been arranged by the stall-holders in beautiful patterns on beds of crushed ice.

In one part of the Ramblas are the sellers of lottery tickets. Britain is about the only country in Europe which does not have a national lottery. In Spain the lottery is as popular as the football pools are in England; there are not many people who do not buy a ticket, or a share in a ticket, every month.

Down by the beach is a long line of open-air fish restaurants where you can eat fish dishes of every description. The tables are shaded by awnings made of split bamboos. To get to the beach, you pass through the kitchens where busy, laughing, singing cooks are busily preparing the dishes.

Not far from the Ramblas are the booths of the letter-writers. Though most young Spaniards go to school and learn to read and write, many of the older people, especially in the country districts, never went to school. They come to the *memorialista*, the professional letter-writers, tell them what they wish to say and have a letter written for them.

In 1928 and 1929 Barcelona held a great exhibition. As part of this exhibition a "Spanish Village" was constructed. A full-sized stone model of every kind of house to be found throughout Spain was built, and working in them are craftsmen from the region from which the house comes.

Barcelona, like all the larger Spanish cities, has its share of beautiful parks and squares where the people promenade in the cool of the day. In the modern city, too, there are broad avenues, the chief of which is a residential street which runs across the upper part of the town to the slopes of another hill called Pedraltes.

One of the features of the city is the Rondas, a semi-circular street which follows the line of the old fortifications. It encloses the old city and the more modern part west of the Ramblas. At the northern point of the Rondas is University Square, through which runs the wide Avenida José Antonio. At each end of this avenue is a bullring. Bullfighting fans say that bullfighting in Barcelona is better than anywhere else in Spain because, instead of being a show for tourists, it is the traditional spectacle which the Spaniards themselves have been attending for centuries.

Barcelona is in the region of Catalonia, and the Catalans are quite different from any other Spaniards. They are proud and independent, and inclined to be rebellious. The Barcelonans have, in fact, often quarrelled with the government in Madrid, when they have objected to what the central authorities decided.

They are rebellious in other ways, too, especially in the arts. Pablo Picasso, who brought about more changes in painting and drawing than any other modern painter, was born in Madrid, and studied there as a young man. Salvador Dali, who was said to paint like a madman, was also a Catalan, as was the architect Antonio Gandi. There is a church of his in Barcelona which looks like a tropical jungle such as H.G. Wells might have imagined it.

Not far from Barcelona is the mountain monastery of

Monserrat. Legend says that the Holy Grail—the cup from which Jesus drank at the Last Supper—was once in the possession of the monks here. However, the monastery still holds a black image of the Virgin Mary, said to have been brought there by St. Peter twenty years after the Crucifixion. Every year thousands of people go to Monserrat to pray and light candles to the Virgin.

Seville and Granada
When foreigners conquer a country and then rule it for

Moorish decoration in Seville's Alcazar palace

several hundred years, they cannot help leaving their mark on it for ever. The Moors have certainly done this in Andalusia, in southern Spain, and especially so in the cities of Seville and Granada. Everywhere you go there are Moorish buildings, like the Giralda bell-tower in Seville, built by the Moors to match others which they had erected in Rabat and Marrakesh in Morocco.

But it is the people of Andalusia who are the most striking feature of the south. The women are darkly beautiful, the men darkly handsome, and all are graceful in their movements. They are what people who have not been to Spain, but have heard how courteous and happy the people are, imagine all Spaniards to be like.

In Andalusia guitars are always playing, castanets clicking and people singing. Here, too, there are more gypsies than anywhere else in Spain, and their encampments seem to be alive with *flamenco* songs and dances.

Seville is one of the most attractive cities in the world. Its winding streets and lanes, enclosed by high walls, link together a host of tiny squares. The centres of these squares are rose-gardens round which people sit for a chat on tiled benches, looking at the wonderful riot of colour and breathing in the fragrance of the flowers. Some of the streets are so narrow that in the day-time, in the summer, awnings are stretched across them to keep out the fierce heat. In the evenings, the awnings are furled back to let in the cool evening air.

From the outside, the houses, with their windows protected

by iron grilles, look rather like prison walls. But as you pass the entrance you will catch a glimpse of the *patio*, or courtyard, crammed full of beautiful flowers. The *patio* is the centre of the home, and flowers are the passion of the people of Seville. Even if a house is small, it will more likely than not have a large garden where the family rest and take pleasure. In the spring the scent of orange blossom mingles with the scent of hundreds of other flowers.

Seville is the fourth largest city in Spain. Most of the buildings have been built in the Moorish style. Even the Christian cathedral, which is the largest church in Europe after St. Peter's in Rome, has a Moorish look about it.

We know Seville chiefly for its oranges, from which we make

73

our marmalade. But there are several industries in the city, too: chocolate, soap, glazed tiles, perfumes and musical instruments. Tobacco products are also made here. It was the Seville tobacco factory, which still stands, that was the scene for Bizet's opera *Carmen*.

Besides the famous Holy Week *fiesta*, Seville has an equally famous fair, the *Feria*, which takes place towards the end of April. For this *casetas*, or tents, are erected and gaily decorated with flowers and festooned with lights. In these *casetas* families entertain their friends and watch the dancing and merry-making which goes on all night.

During the six days of the *Feria* Seville does not seem to sleep at all. By day there are parades in which hundreds of men on horseback take part, dressed in leather trousers, short jackets and wide-brimmed hats. Girls dressed in flowered dresses, their black hair beautifully dressed and decorated with bows

A carriage in a parade during the "Feria"

A view of Granada with the Sierra Nevada in the background

and combs, ride behind the men or in carriages. Then, during the night, the guitars and the castanets strike up and the dancers stamp and whirl to the songs and clapping of the onlookers.

Still in Andalusia, but 240 kilometres (a hundred and fifty miles) east of Seville, perched 600 metres (2,000 feet) above the sea, is Granada. Behind it tower the peaks of the Sierra Nevada, rising to 3,478 metres (11,400 feet). (The word *sierra* is used here to mean "mountain range" but primarily it means

75

"saw teeth". If you see a whole range of mountains, the peaks which rise out of it do look like the teeth of a saw.)

Granada is the most Moorish city in Spain. It was here that the Moorish kings lived in their fabulous palace called the Alhambra. It was here, too, that they made their last stand in the fifteenth century when Ferdinand of Aragon and Isabella of Castile at last succeeded in driving the Moors out of Spain after nearly eight hundred years of rule.

The Alhambra was a fortress as well as a palace. The outside walls are of great thickness and strength, but once you have passed these barriers, you enter a fairyland of the most delicate architecture imaginable.

The main entrance to the Alhambra is the Gate of Justice. Sitting here, the Moorish kings listened to the petitions of their people. The gate is formed of two arches. Over the outer arch is carved an open hand, and over the inner arch a key. A Moorish legend said that the Christians would never take the Alhambra until the open hand grasped the key.

The halls, chambers and smaller courts of the palace are grouped around two giant courts, the Court of the Lions and the Court of the Fishponds. The Court of the Lions gets its name from the twelve marble lions grouped round the fountain in the centre. The Court of the Fishponds is 46 metres (roughly 150 feet) long and the whole of it is filled by a marble bath. It is difficult, if not impossible, to describe the special beauty of the Alhambra in words.

The other feature of Granada which visitors find interesting

The Court of the Lions in the Alhambra

is the large number of gypsies who live in the caves in the hillsides around the city. Some of these caves are really elaborate homes with electric light, telephones and modern furniture. The gypsies make the greater part of their living from entertaining tourists with their songs and dances.

Toledo

Toledo was once the capital city of Spain. It stands on the River Tagus and is only seventy-six kilometres (forty-seven miles) by railway from Madrid.

In ancient times, Toledo was famous for its swordmakers. Toledo steel was the best in the world. The Moors introduced the art of damascening—the word comes from the name

77

Gypsies entertaining tourists in Granada. The cave in which they are dancing has been modernised for this purpose

Damascus—the hilts and scabbards of their swords here. *Damascening* is making patterns by beating threads of gold and silver into the steel.

Toledo steel is still of very high quality. Nowadays, instead of producing swords, Toledo makes scissors and knives which are sent all over the world. There is also a considerable tourist trade in miniature swords which can be used as paper-knives.

When El Greco came to Spain from Italy in about 1575, he settled in Toledo and lived there for the rest of his life.

The old city is built on a rock high above the waters of the River Tagus which runs almost completely round it. It is said

78

that Toledo steel is so fine because there are special properties in the water of the Tagus. The steel is plunged red-hot into the water to temper it; that is, to bring it to its required hardness. The blade of a Toledo sword never breaks, yet if you put the point in the floor, you can bend the hilt down to the floor also, so that the blade forms a circle.

Toledo has a magnificent cathedral. The Cardinal Archbishop of all Spain has always lived there, and still does today, ruling the Church with all the pomp of a medieval prince.

Cadiz
Cadiz is one of the oldest ports in the world. Said to have been founded by the Phoenicians in about 1180 B.C. on a peninsula on the south-west coast of Spain jutting out into the Atlantic, by 700 B.C. it was a famous market for tin, silver and amber. Yet during the Middle Ages it disappeared from the pages of history.

When Alfonso X of Castile recaptured Cadiz from the Moors in 1262, there were scarcely any Spaniards living there, and the king had to send people to settle there. It was not until Columbus discovered America that the port began to be prosperous again. Two hundred years later, despite the fact that it was often attacked by pirates, it was a far wealthier port than London.

In 1587, when the ships for the great Armada against England had been built, Philip II collected them all in Cadiz harbour, so that they could be fitted out and loaded with supplies. Shortly before they were ready to sail, Sir Francis Drake and his ships attacked them and burnt many of them with fire-ships. Drake called it, "singeing the King of Spain's beard".

A great part of the old town was burned down in 1596, and the public buildings of Cadiz are now mostly modern. It has two cathedrals, a picture gallery, a library and museum and, of course, a bullring. Many people call it the Venice of Spain, because there are no motor-cars, and so no noise or fumes and, from almost every point in the city, you can see the sea.

Eighty kilometres (about fifty miles) south-east of Cadiz, is

The port of Cadiz

A "bodega" in which sherry casks are stored

Cape Trafalgar, where Nelson defeated the French fleets in 1805.

Jerez

There are two cities in Spain called Jerez—Jerez de la Frontera and Jerez de los Caballeros. Although the second was the birthplace of Vasco Nunez de Balboa, who discovered the Pacific Ocean, Jerez de la Frontera is the more famous of the two. It is here that sherry, the world-famous Spanish wine, is made. "Sherry" is the English way of pronouncing Jerez.

Jerez de la Frontera, which is forty-eight kilometres (thirty miles) by railway north-north-east of Cadiz, is surrounded by vineyards—which produce the wine—olive groves and large pastures for horses. It is quite a large town with nearly 200,000 inhabitants.

The grapes are gathered in September and taken to the farms in ox-carts. Then they are spread out on rush mats in the yards and left to lie in the sun. The heat of the sun makes them very ripe and increases the sugar in them.

For "dry" (unsweet) sherry, the grapes are left in the sun for twenty-four hours, but for "sweet" sherry they are left for about two weeks. They are then gathered up and placed in huge vats. Men, wearing leather boots with hobnails in the soles, tread on the grapes and squeeze the juice out of them.

The juice is left in the vats to ferment. When it is ready, it is drawn off into huge oak casks, which are stood in cool warehouses, known as *bodegas*. After some time in the casks, it is sold.

When the grape harvest has been gathered and the grapes crushed, all the people of Jerez take part in a great *fiesta*.

Corunna

Spain's other important port on the Atlantic coast is Corunna in the north. Like Cadiz, it stands on a peninsula.

The old town is protected by a citadel and walls. The large modern town has arsenals and barracks, and a cable station which carries many trans-Atlantic telegrams.

There are no dockyards in Corunna. It is just a port, but a very busy and thriving one. In the town there are canning

Corunna—gardens in the city centre

factories for fish and vegetables, and these provide most of the business for the port. For example, nearly all the tins of sardines exported by Spain pass through Corunna.

When the British were fighting Napoleon in Spain during the Peninsular War, Sir John Moore, the British commander in Portugal, marched north to join up with Spanish troops. Napoleon quickly collected an army to crush the English.

Moore, whose army was not very strong, quickly realised

Corunna—a view of the fishing harbour and a street of houses with glass-fronted balconies

that he was in great danger from these French forces, and decided to retreat towards Corunna, where he ordered his fleet to meet him and rescue his wounded soldiers.

While the wounded were being taken on board, the French attacked. During the battle, Sir John Moore was seriously wounded, and later died. He was buried in Corunna, where his tomb can still be seen.

Perhaps you know the poem by Charles Wolfe, which begins

> *Not a drum was heard, not a funeral note,*
> *As his corse to the rampart we hurried.*

It describes the burial of Sir John Moore at Corunna.

Majorca, Minorca, Ibiza
and the Canary Islands

Lying off the east coast of Spain is a group of islands called the Balearics, (pronounced *Bally-arricks*). The three larger islands in this group are Majorca, Minorca and Ibiza (pronounced *Ibee-tha*).

These islands have become very popular with holiday-makers in the last thirty years, especially Majorca and Ibiza. The reason for this popularity is that, even compared with the simple way of life and low cost of living in Spain, the islands provide wonderful holidays, at a low cost, for people anxious to escape from the hurly-burly of the modern world.

Another reason is that, being islands, the weather is not so hot there in summer as it is on the mainland in Spain. Sea breezes take much of the heat out of the sun.

Majorca is the largest of the islands. Palma, its capital, is a beautiful and interesting little city. Rain very seldom falls there, and then only for a few days in the early spring or late autumn. A long northern range of mountains protects Palma from the cold winds that blow down from the Pyrenees. Because of this it is possible to grow semi-tropical fruit and flowers. Luxurious vegetation can be seen everywhere.

85

On Ibiza life used to be more simple and cheaper even than on Majorca. But when foreign visitors began to go there, the Spaniards built modern hotels which have spoiled the simplicity of the place.

Minorca is not so popular as the other two islands. The main reason is that a wind always blows there which makes it a more bleak and less attractive place.

The Canary Islands, in the Atlantic, 1045 kilometres (650 miles) from Europe but only 115 kilometres (seventy-two

Cala Portinatx, Ibiza

Porto Cristo, Majorca

miles) from the north-west coast of Africa, also belong to Spain. Quite a number of people holiday there, because the climate, even at Christmas, is warmer.

Lastly, there is Spanish Morocco, a strip of country along the North African coast, surrounding the port of Tangier, which is an international port; that is, it belongs to nobody and everybody at the same time. Tangier is a renowned centre for modern smugglers, especially of tobacco and cigarettes.

The Basques

The Basque country lies in the north-east corner of Spain, under the Pyrenees. There are Spanish Basques and French Basques. That is to say, the frontier between France and Spain runs through the Basque country; but though split in two like this, there is no difference between the people on one side of the frontier and the other, except that the French Basques have become French, while the Spanish Basques have remained Basque.

The Spanish Basques are quite different from any other Spaniards. Like all people who live in hilly country, they are thickset and have slightly bow legs. They are athletic; they invented *pelota*, and one of their favourite pastimes is running up and down mountains. They are hearty people, who like eating and drinking and, above all, talking—in their own Basque language, which has no resemblance to Spanish, and which few people who are not Basques can speak.

They are very independent people, too, and often quarrel with the government in Madrid. They want to be a country on their own, but Madrid does not agree, although in 1978 it gave them the right to govern themselves. Many of them are not satisfied with that and are aiming to win complete independence.

Whether they will soon get their wish, it is difficult to say; but if they do not, it will not be for want of trying.

88

Gibraltar

Many thousands of years ago, Africa was joined to Spain. In time the sea wore away the land between the two countries where the present Straits of Gibraltar join the Atlantic with the Mediterranean. At their narrowest point, the Straits are only fourteen kilometres (nine miles) wide, less than half the distance between Dover and Calais, across the Straits of Dover.

On either side of the Straits of Gibraltar are what are really two mountains which the ancient Greeks and Romans used to call the Pillars of Hercules. On the African side is Mount Abyla; on the Spanish side, the Rock of Gibraltar.

The Rock is actually at the seaward end of a narrow peninsula which joins it to the mainland. On the westward side is a sheltered bay which provides Gibraltar with a fine natural harbour.

A glance at the map will show you that anyone who is in possession of Gibraltar controls the only entrance to the Mediterranean. It was because of this that in 1704 Britain decided to seize the Rock, in order to stop the Spanish and French fleets from becoming masters of the Mediterranean.

Since that day, 24th July 1704, Gibraltar has been a British colony. The Spaniards have made several unsuccessful attempts to get it back over the years. Today the Spanish government is demanding the return of the Rock, and it seems possible that one day Britain will have to hand it back. But the main difficulty in reaching an agreement is that the 30,000

Gibraltar, seen from the sea

people who live in the tiny colony consider themselves to be British, and do not wish to be governed by Madrid.

During the Second World War, after the defeat of France, Gibraltar became the British naval base in the western Mediterranean. The Rock was more strongly fortified than ever. Underground stores, air-raid shelters, hospitals and barracks were tunnelled out of the Rock, and the race-course was turned into an air-field. Quite a number of British secret agents were flown to Gibraltar, and from there taken by submarine or small fishing-boat and landed on the south coast of France.

Spain's Place in the World

For some years after the end of the Second World War, Spain passed through a very difficult time. The United Nations refused to admit her as a member, because it was believed that she had helped the Germans secretly during the war. The United States also refused to help with much-needed money.

The object of this unfriendliness was to try to make the Spaniards replace General Franco's government by a more democratic form of rule. The exact opposite happened. The majority of Spaniards stood more firmly behind Franco than ever.

These modern blocks in Palma, Majorca, show how quickly Spain is catching up with the more prosperous nations of Europe

When this was realised, the other countries changed their attitudes. Spain was admitted to the United Nations (1955) and she was asked to join in the plan for the defence of western Europe. This she agreed to do and, in return for bases for the American Air Force, the United States made her loans of several hundreds of millions of dollars.

These loans helped Spain to expand her industries and to increase her exports. With the money she earns from exports, and the large sums which the tourists bring into the country, Spain has been able to become a much more up-to-date country.

Though only a shadow of the great, world-wide empire of the sixteenth century, modern Spain is quickly catching up with the prosperous nations of Europe, and may do so even more quickly now that democratic parliamentary government seems to have become firmly established.

Index

93